GRAPHIC SCIENCE

LESSONS IN SCIENCE SAFETY

WITH MAX AXIOM SUPER SCIENTIST

An Augmented Reading Science Experience

by Donald B. Lemke and Thomas K. Adamson | illustrated by Tod Smith and Bill Anderson

Consultant:
Dr. Ronald Browne
Associate Professor of Elementary Education
Minnesota State University, Mankato

CAPSTONE PRESS
a capstone imprint

Graphic Library is published by Capstone Press,
1710 Roe Crest Drive, North Mankato, Minnesota 56003.
www.mycapstone.com

Library of Congress Cataloging-in-Publication Data is available on the Library of
Congress website.

ISBN: 978-1-5435-2948-7 (library binding)
ISBN: 978-1-5435-2959-3 (paperback)
ISBN: 978-1-5435-2969-2 (eBook PDF)

Summary: In graphic novel format, follows the adventures of Max Axiom as
he explains the importance of science safety.

Art Director and Designer
Bob Lentz

Colorist
Otha Zackariah Edward Lohse

Cover Artist
Tod Smith

Editor
Christopher L. Harbo

Photo Credits
Capstone Studio/Karon Dubke: 29

Download the Capstone app!

- Ask an adult to download the Capstone 4D app.

- Scan the cover and stars inside the book for additional content.

When you scan a spread, you'll find fun extra stuff
to go with this book! You can also find these things
on the web at www.capstone4D.com using the
password: safety.29487

TABLE OF CONTENTS

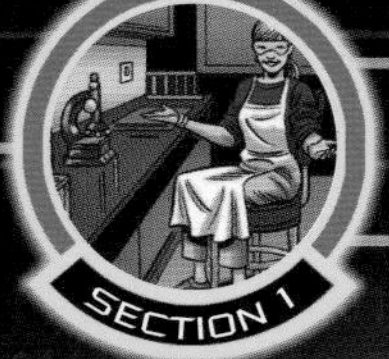
SECTION 1

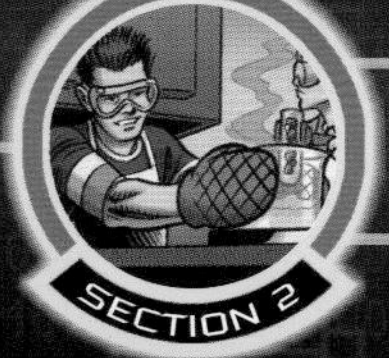
SECTION 2

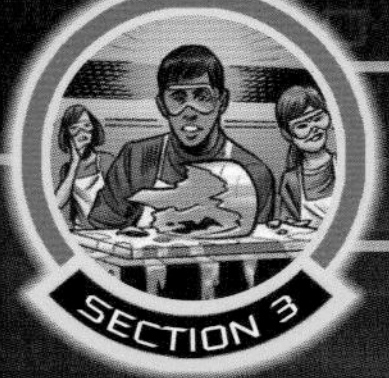
SECTION 3

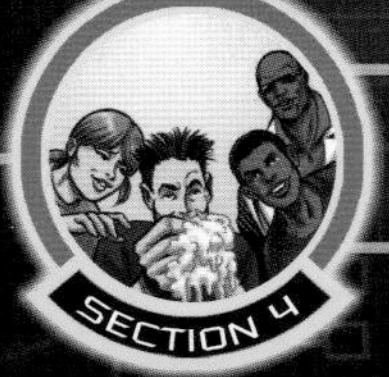
SECTION 4

SECTION 1 PREPARING FOR THE LAB

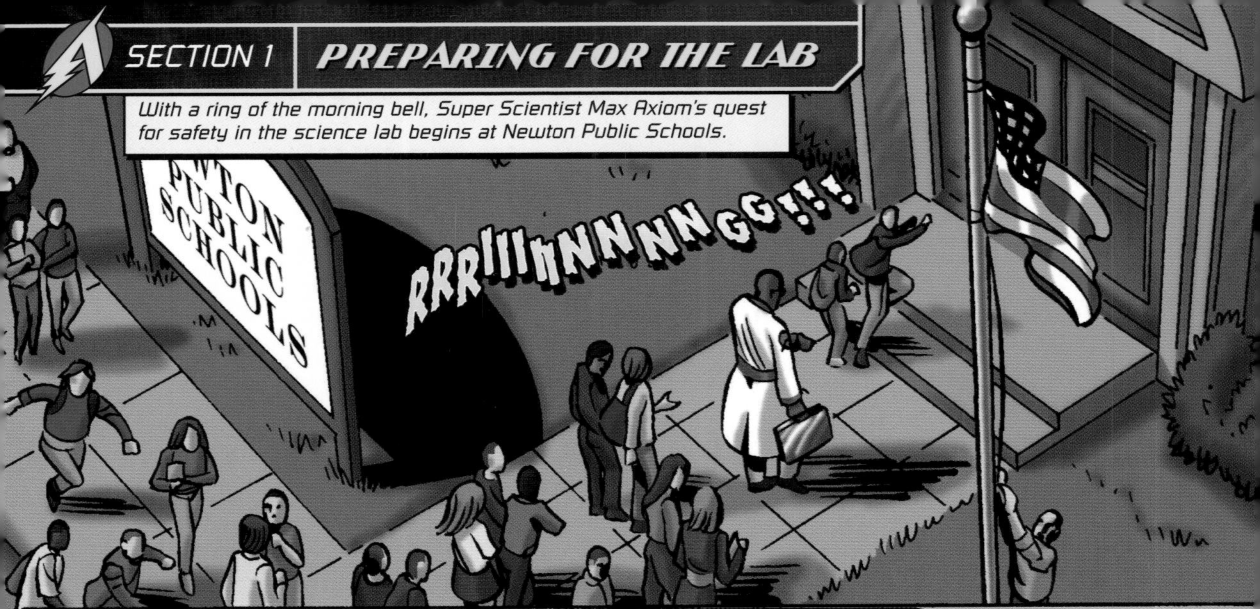

With a ring of the morning bell, Super Scientist Max Axiom's quest for safety in the science lab begins at Newton Public Schools.
WTON PUBLIC SCHOOLS
RRRIIIINNNNNGG!!!

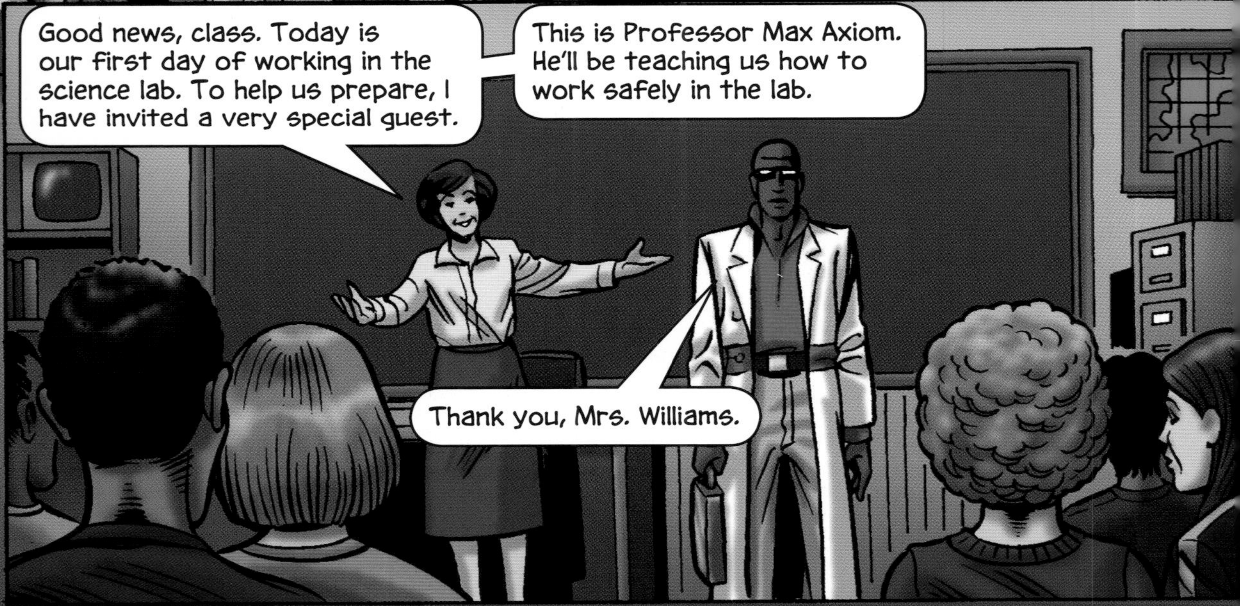

Good news, class. Today is our first day of working in the science lab. To help us prepare, I have invited a very special guest.
This is Professor Max Axiom. He'll be teaching us how to work safely in the lab.
Thank you, Mrs. Williams.

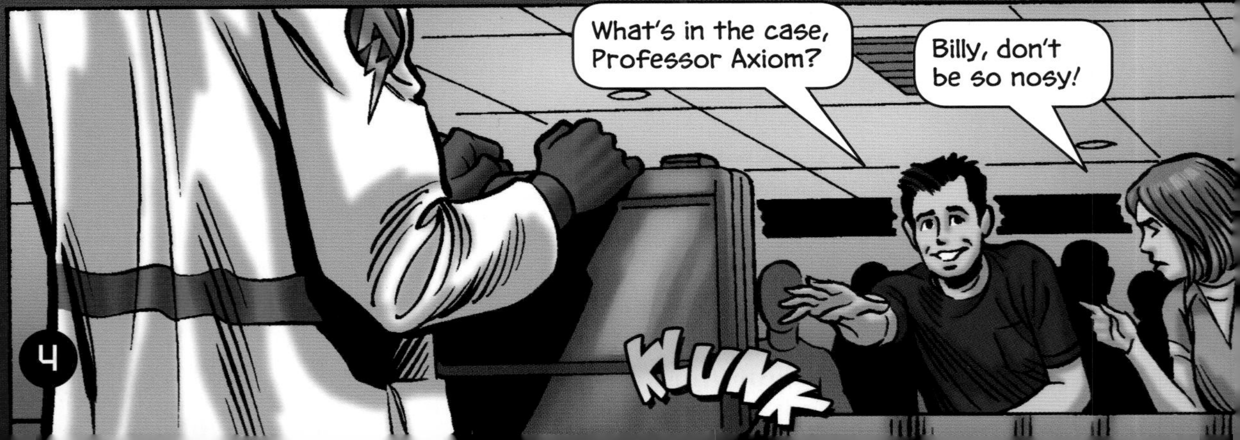

What's in the case, Professor Axiom?
Billy, don't be so nosy!
KLUNK

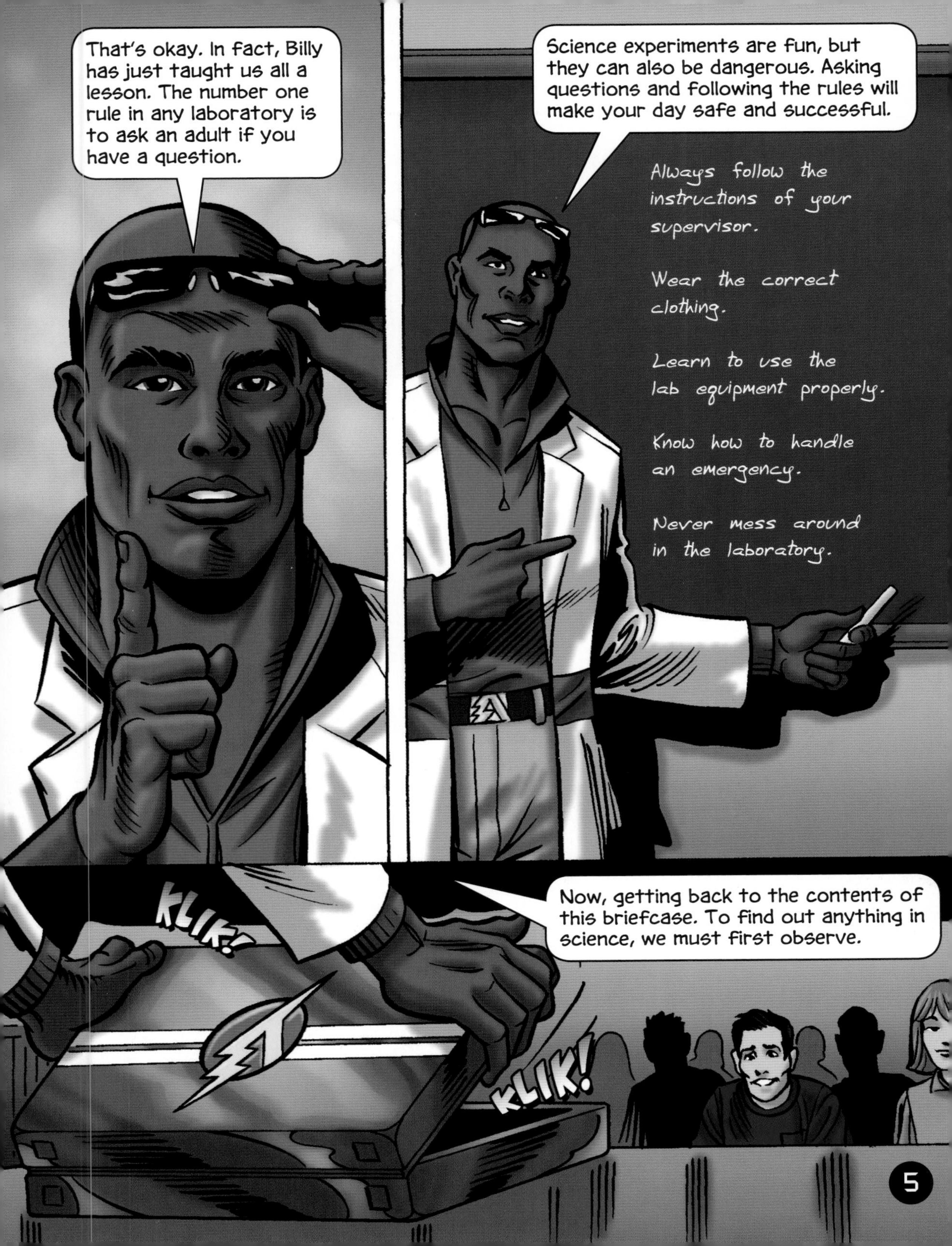
That's okay. In fact, Billy has just taught us all a lesson. The number one rule in any laboratory is to ask an adult if you have a question.
Science experiments are fun, but they can also be dangerous. Asking questions and following the rules will make your day safe and successful.
Always follow the instructions of your supervisor.
Wear the correct clothing.
Learn to use the lab equipment properly.
Know how to handle an emergency.
Never mess around in the laboratory.
KLIK!
Now, getting back to the contents of this briefcase. To find out anything in science, we must first observe.
KLIK!

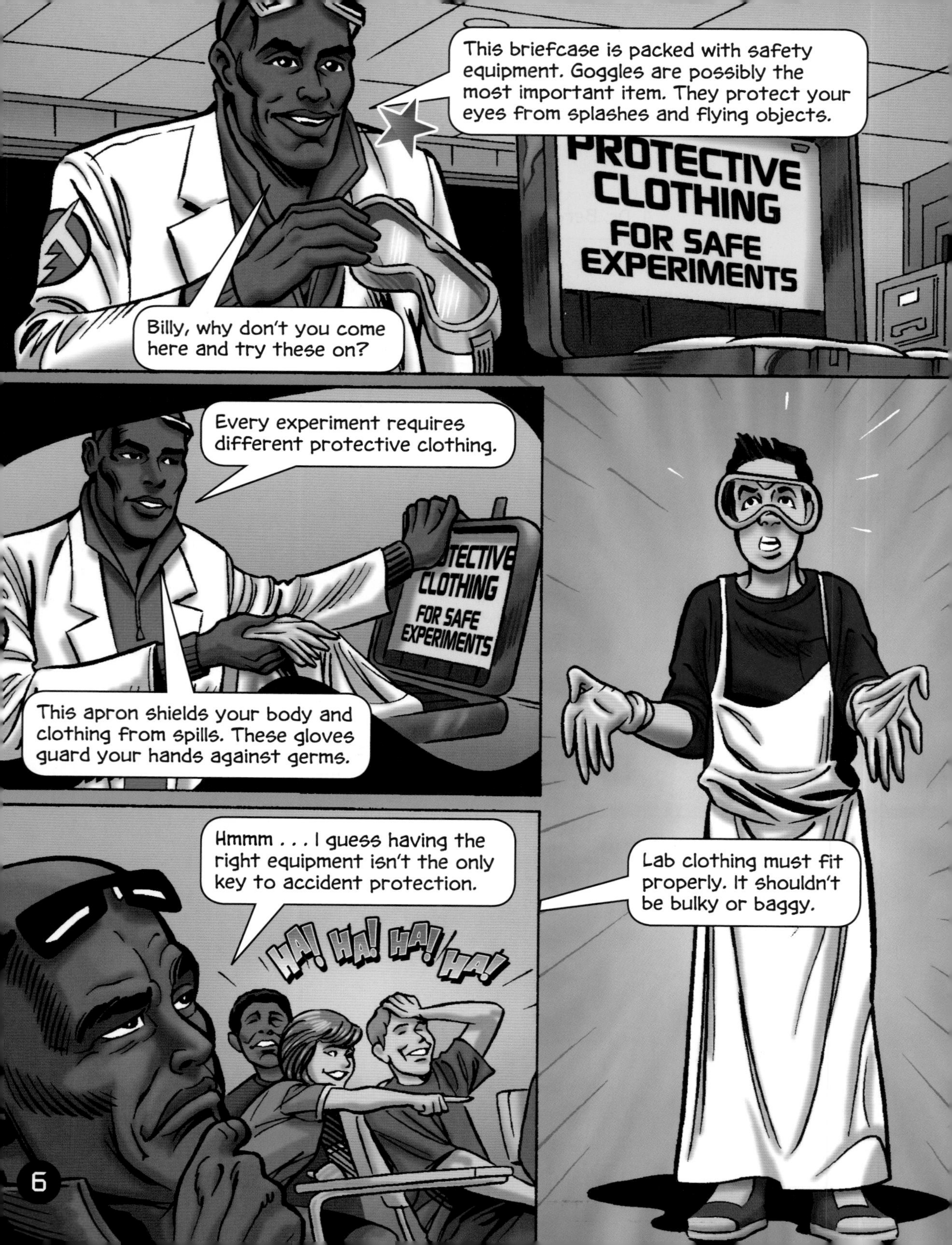
This briefcase is packed with safety equipment. Goggles are possibly the most important item. They protect your eyes from splashes and flying objects.
PROTECTIVE CLOTHING FOR SAFE EXPERIMENTS
Billy, why don't you come here and try these on?
Every experiment requires different protective clothing.
PROTECTIVE CLOTHING FOR SAFE EXPERIMENTS
This apron shields your body and clothing from spills. These gloves guard your hands against germs.
Lab clothing must fit properly. It shouldn't be bulky or baggy.
Hmmm . . . I guess having the right equipment isn't the only key to accident protection.
HA! HA! HA! HA!

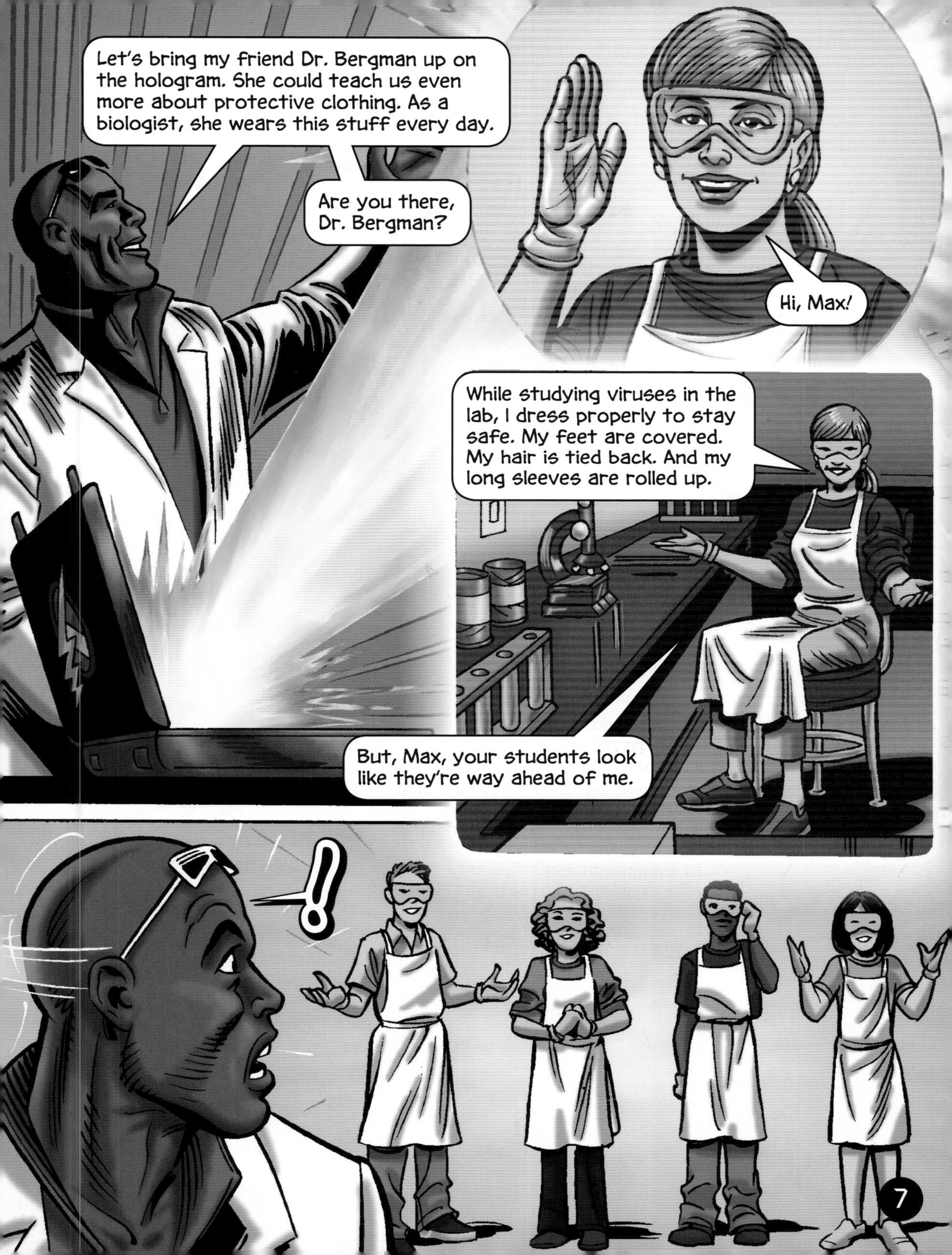

Let's bring my friend Dr. Bergman up on the hologram. She could teach us even more about protective clothing. As a biologist, she wears this stuff every day.
Are you there, Dr. Bergman?
Hi, Max!
While studying viruses in the lab, I dress properly to stay safe. My feet are covered. My hair is tied back. And my long sleeves are rolled up.
But, Max, your students look like they're way ahead of me.
!

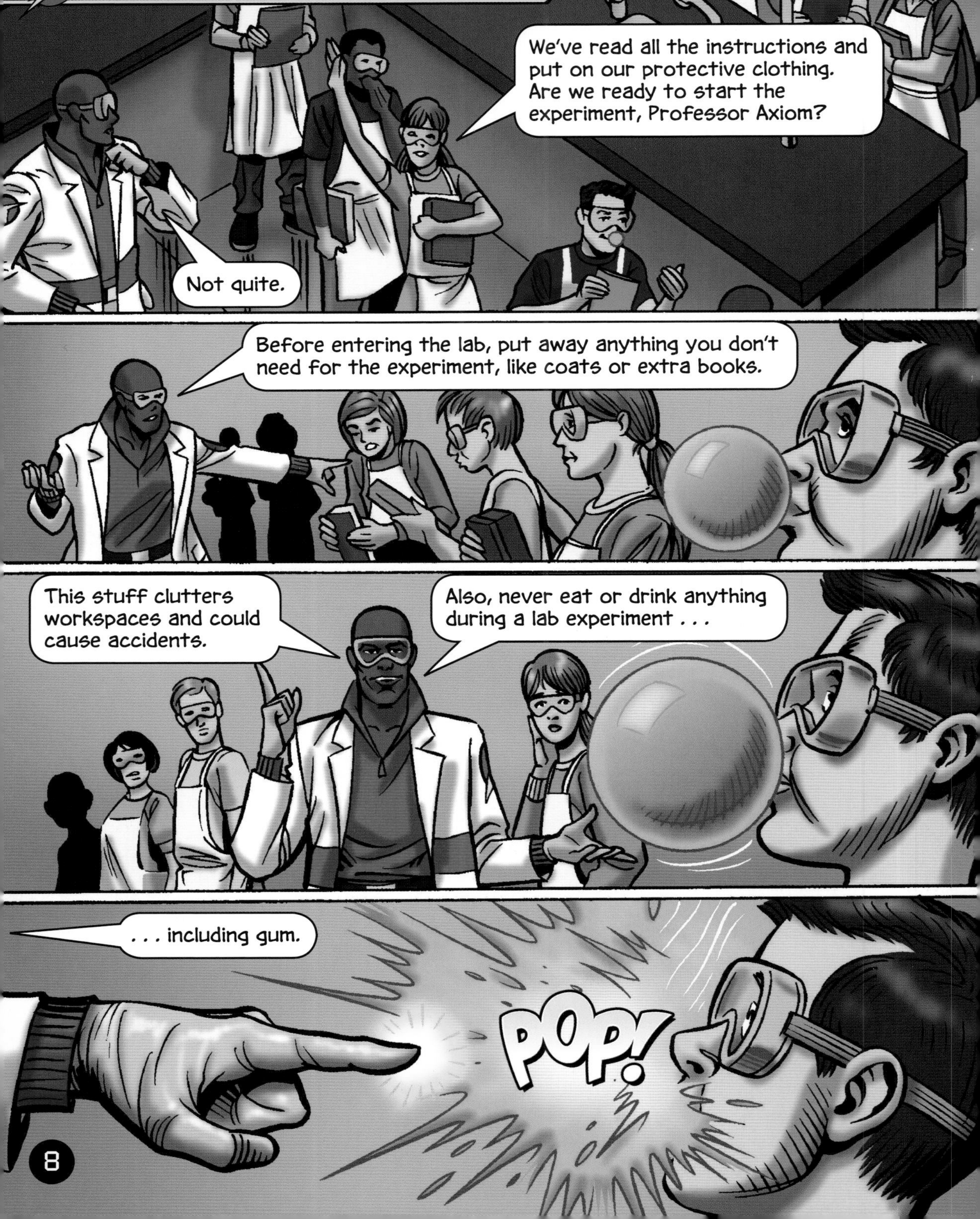
We've read all the instructions and put on our protective clothing. Are we ready to start the experiment, Professor Axiom?
Not quite.
Before entering the lab, put away anything you don't need for the experiment, like coats or extra books.
This stuff clutters workspaces and could cause accidents.
Also, never eat or drink anything during a lab experiment . . .
. . . including gum.
POP!

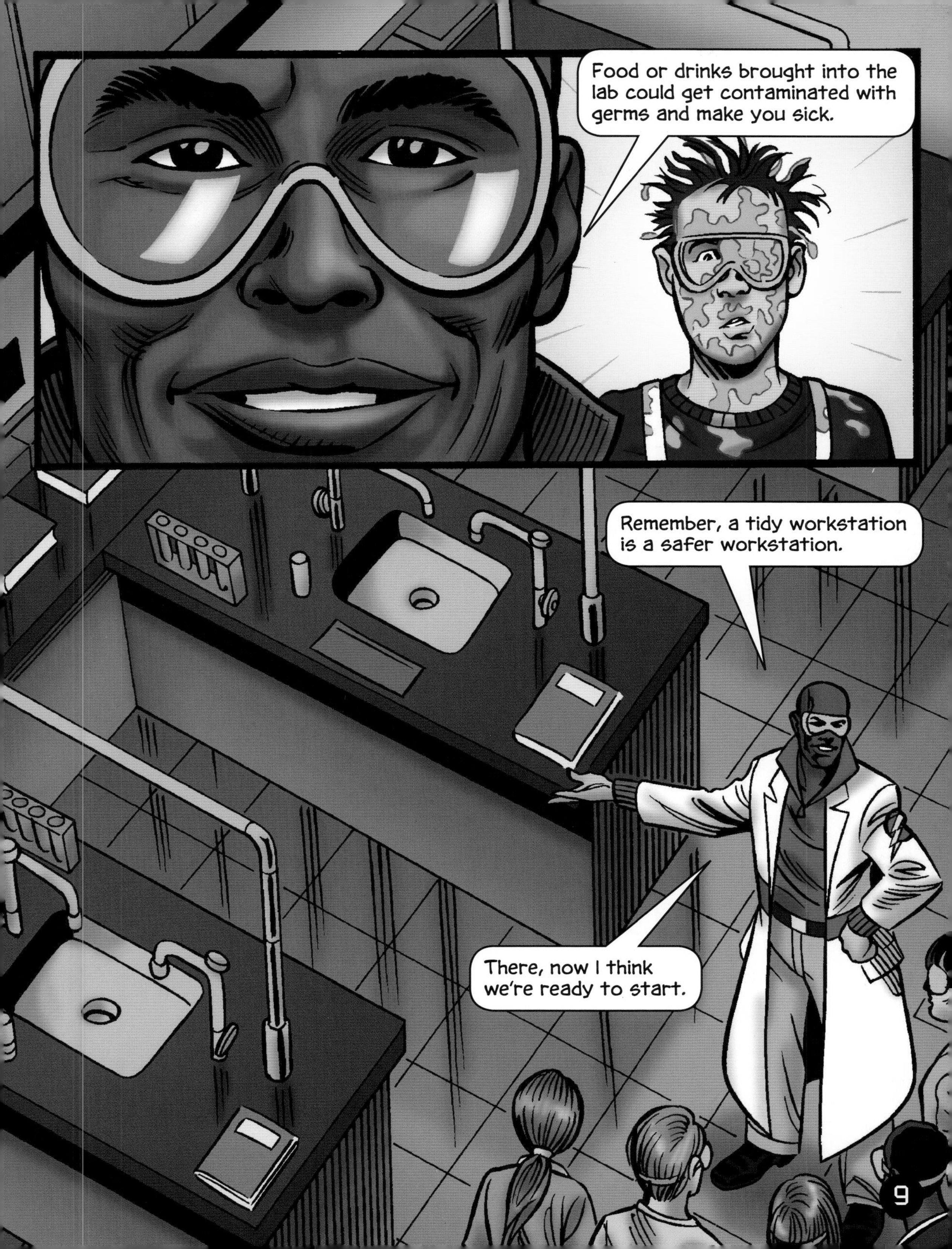
Food or drinks brought into the lab could get contaminated with germs and make you sick.
Remember, a tidy workstation is a safer workstation.
There, now I think we're ready to start.

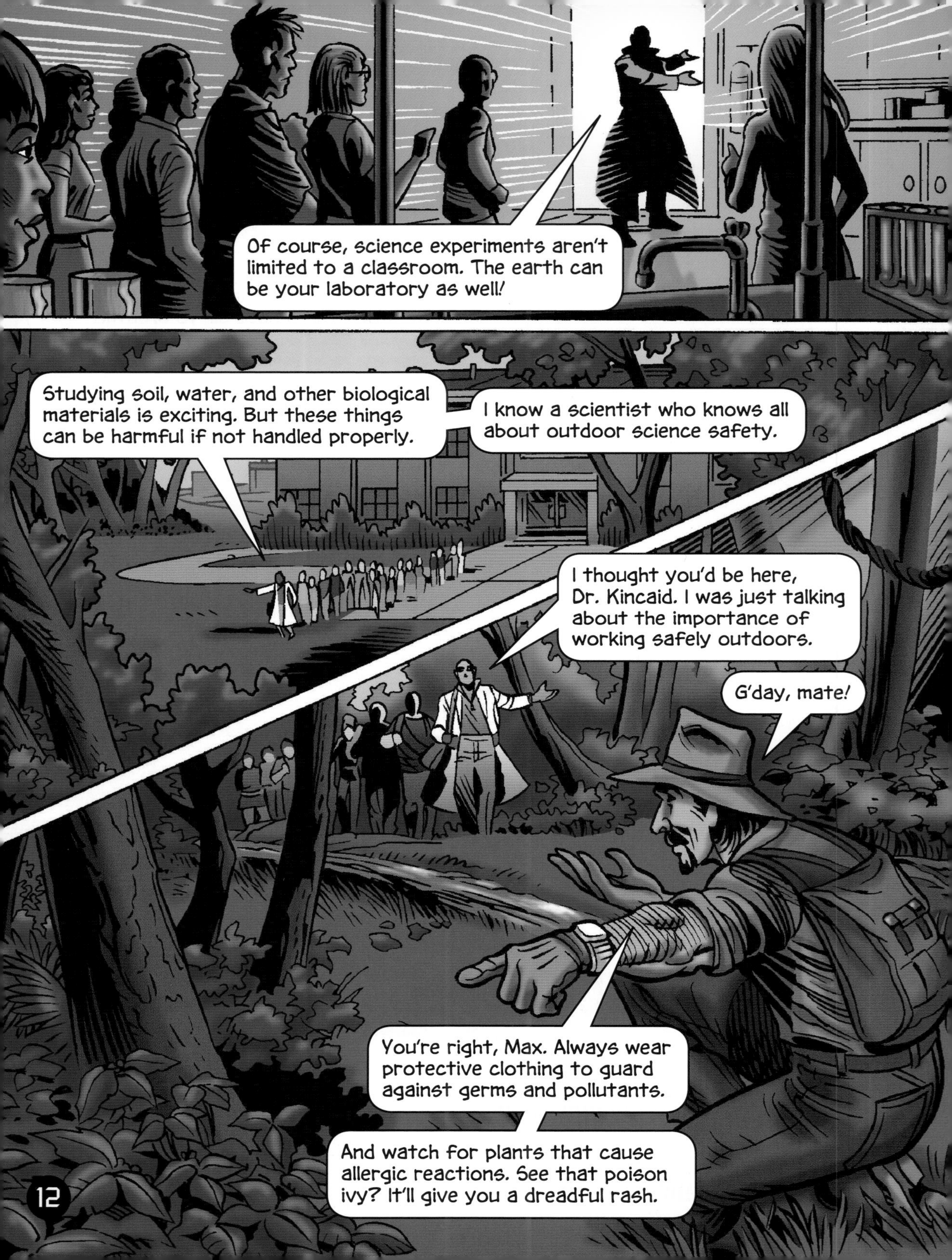
Of course, science experiments aren't limited to a classroom. The earth can be your laboratory as well!
Studying soil, water, and other biological materials is exciting. But these things can be harmful if not handled properly.
I know a scientist who knows all about outdoor science safety.
I thought you'd be here, Dr. Kincaid. I was just talking about the importance of working safely outdoors.
G'day, mate!
You're right, Max. Always wear protective clothing to guard against germs and pollutants.
And watch for plants that cause allergic reactions. See that poison ivy? It'll give you a dreadful rash.

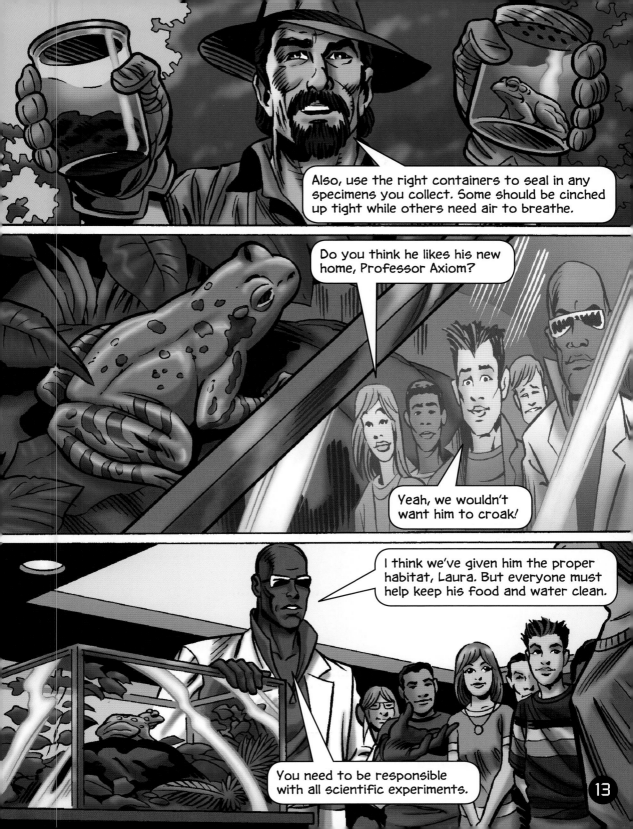

Dr. Lopez?

Hi, Max. I'm testing a sticky lollipop mixture.

I have to stay here and watch it heat up. We never leave a heat source unattended.

I'm testing different flavors to see how higher heat affects each one.

149° C

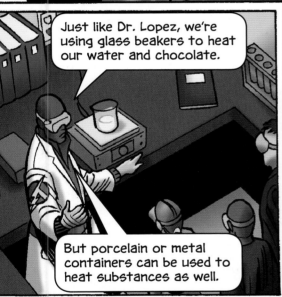

Just like Dr. Lopez, we're using glass beakers to heat our water and chocolate.

But porcelain or metal containers can be used to heat substances as well.

Whatever container is used, it should have a label that says "heat resistant."

HEAT RESISTANT

Looks like your water is ready for the next step in this experiment.

Professor Axiom!

Uh-oh. I better see what's going on over there.

Quick, dude, clean it up!

Wait just a minute! We need to treat all spills in the lab the same, whether it's a chemical or something as harmless as water. And I'll bet the hot plate is still hot, isn't it?

Yes, it's still on and plugged in.

All right. Proceed carefully because an electric shock is possible if you touch a wet appliance that's still on.

Not to mention the danger of all this broken glass.

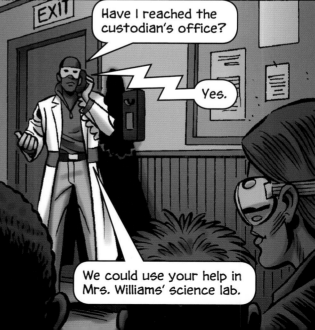

Have I reached the custodian's office?

Yes.

We could use your help in Mrs. Williams' science lab.

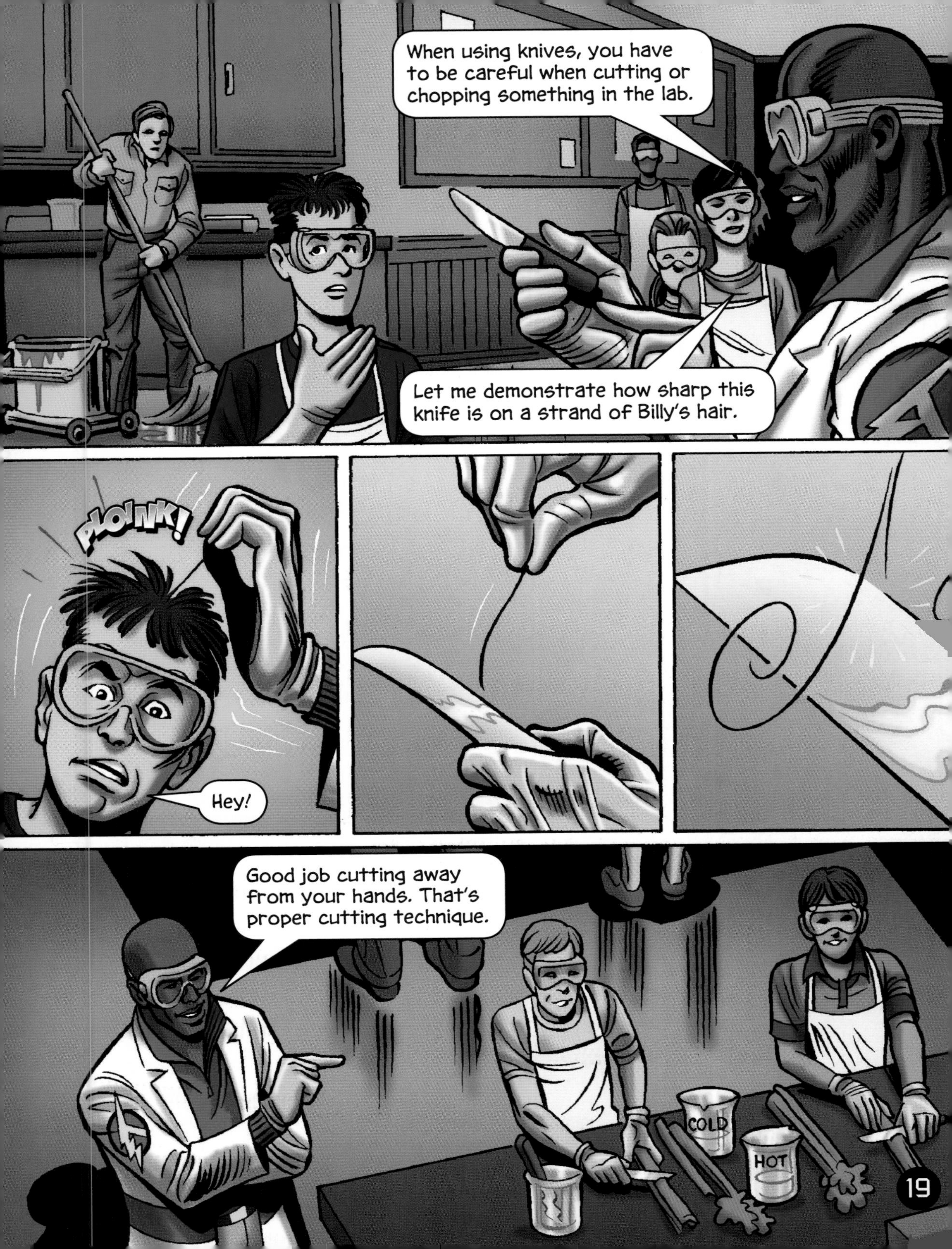
When using knives, you have to be careful when cutting or chopping something in the lab.
Let me demonstrate how sharp this knife is on a strand of Billy's hair.
PLOINK!
Hey!
Good job cutting away from your hands. That's proper cutting technique.
COLD
HOT

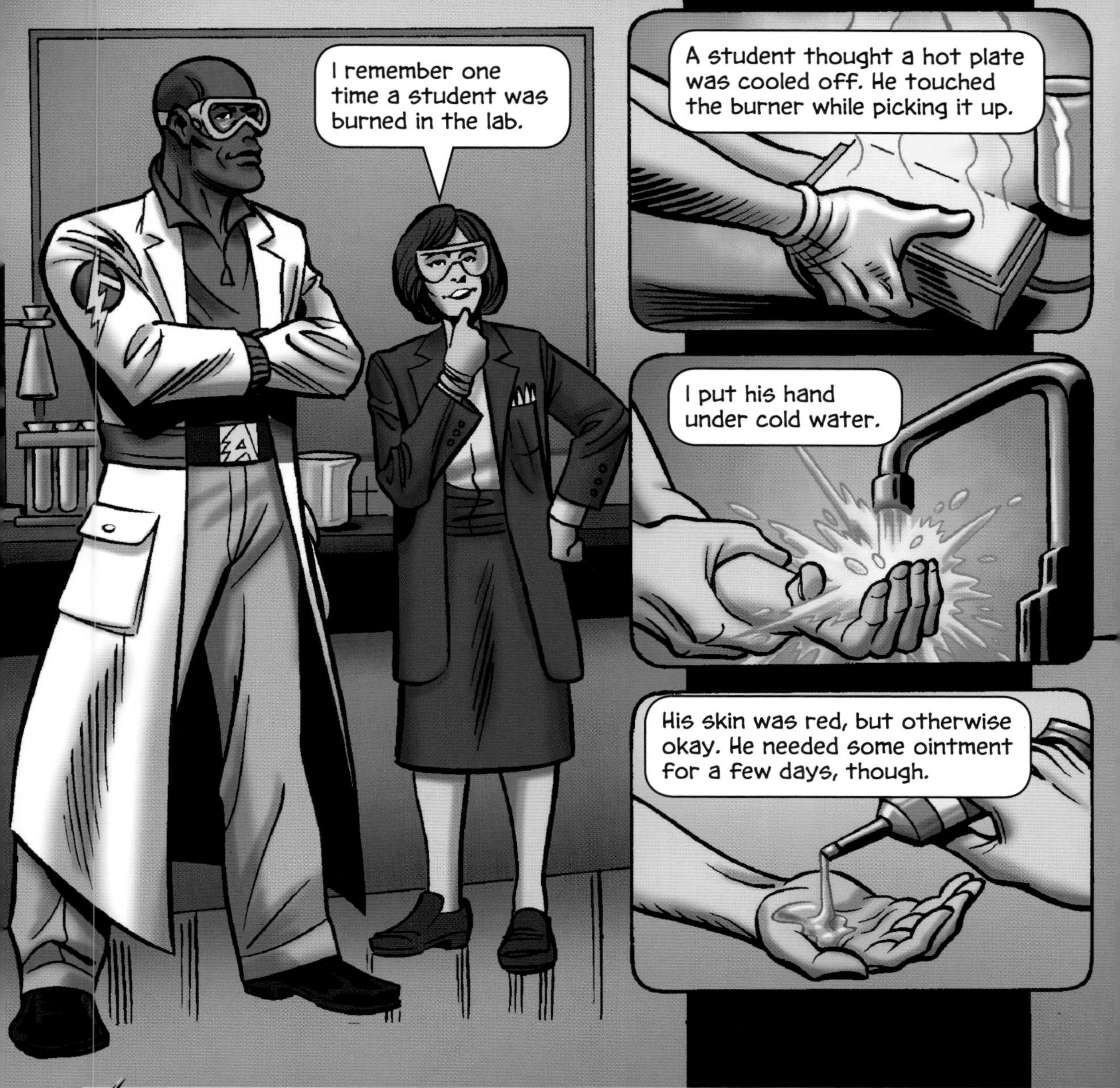
I remember one time a student was burned in the lab.
A student thought a hot plate was cooled off. He touched the burner while picking it up.
I put his hand under cold water.
His skin was red, but otherwise okay. He needed some ointment for a few days, though.

STOP, DROP, AND ROLL

ACCESS GRANTED: MAX AXIOM

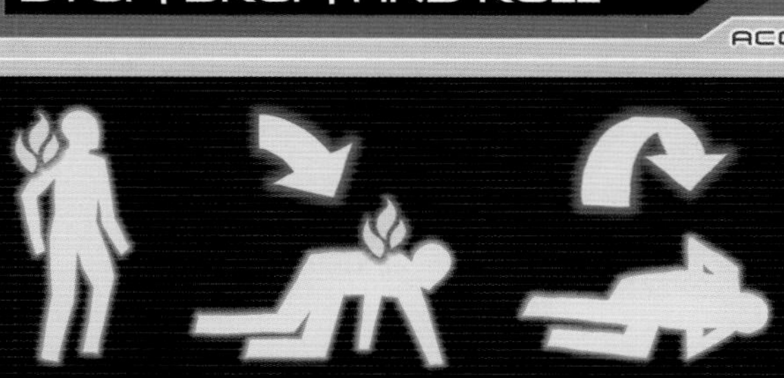

If your clothes catch fire, you need to put out the flames fast. Three simple steps can save your life. Stop what you are doing. Drop to the ground. Roll your body to smother the flames.

SCIENCE SAFETY

Before beginning a lab experiment, be sure you understand the instructions completely. Ask questions if you don't understand. If the instructions are written, read them carefully and follow each step exactly. If you have any questions during the experiment, ask your teacher.

They may not be fashionable, but safety goggles must be worn at all times in the lab. For the best protection, use goggles that shield your eyes from both chemical splashes and flying objects. These goggles are always labeled with the code ANSI Z87.1.

Right now your body has more germs on it than there are people living in the United States! Washing your hands for at least 20 seconds is the best way to prevent millions of germs from passing to your mouth, nose, and eyes.

Environmental scientists test soil and water for pollutants. In 1989, the *Exxon Valdez* crashed and spilled oil into Prince William Sound, Alaska. Wearing protective clothing, environmental scientists helped determine the best cleanup methods. With their help, the area is slowly returning to a healthy environment.

Learning about animals is fun, but handle lab animals only if your teacher gives you permission. If a lab animal bites or scratches you, be sure to tell your teacher immediately. Also, wash your hands before and after you handle an animal. Washing hands protects you from passing germs to or receiving germs from the animal.

Scientists studying erupting volcanoes sometimes wear silver full body suits. These suits have a metal coating that reflects the intense heat of molten lava. Scientists studying sharks sometimes wear shark suits when diving. These suits are made of a steel mesh that protects against shark bites.

Some protective gloves are made of latex. This material can cause an allergic reaction in some people. If you experience a rash or itching while wearing latex gloves, tell your supervisor.

LAB SAFETY MANUAL

Craft your very own manual of procedures, precautions, and preventative measures that help you—and your lab mates—follow science's golden rule: Safety first!

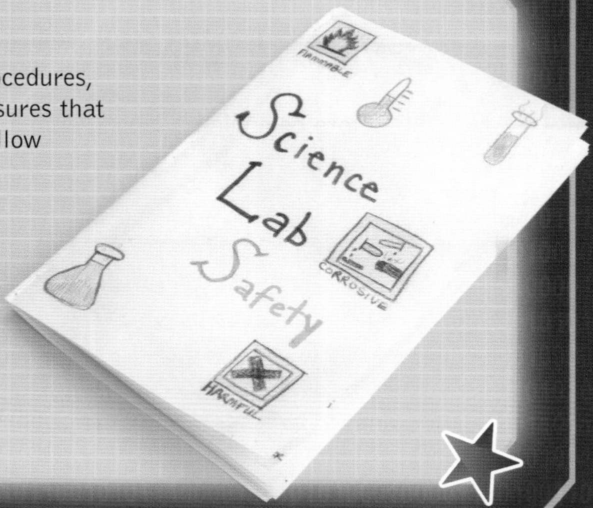
FLAMMABLE
Science
Lab
Safety
CORROSIVE
HARMFUL

WHAT YOU NEED:

- notepad
- pencil
- printer paper
- stapler
- crayons and markers

WHAT YOU DO:

1. Ask a teacher to show you around the school science lab.
2. Make a list in your notepad of the safety equipment you see. Ask your teacher how to use it and write down what you learn.
3. Recall the information you read about science safety. Can you make a list of the potential hazards and important safety procedures for your lab?
4. Stack several sheets of printer paper and fold them in half. The packet of paper should now look like a booklet.
5. Staple along the booklet's spine three or four times to hold the pages together.
6. Make the booklet into a useful safety manual for your school's science lab. Use crayons and markers to write and draw the following information in your manual:
   - Lab hazards to avoid and how to handle them.
   - Safety equipment available, how it's used, and where it's found. You could even draw a map!
   - Safety procedures to remember and specific steps for following them.
7. Label and decorate the cover of your science lab safety manual and illustrate the manual as you see fit.
8. When you're finished, take your safety manual with you—but remember to bring it back each time you visit the lab!

DISCUSSION QUESTIONS

1. You should always dry your hands before unplugging a power cord. What dangers does this prevent?

2. Your choice of clothing can affect a lab activity. What safety precaution should you take if you are wearing long sleeves?

3. Why isn't chewing gum allowed in a science laboratory? Discuss three reasons why.

4. Wafting is a safe technique for smelling chemicals in the science lab. How is wafting done, and when should it be used?

WRITING PROMPTS

1. What should you do if your clothing catches on fire in the lab? List the steps to take and write a sentence or two explaining how to do each one.

2. The right clothes are essential for lab safety. Make a list of things to wear for safety if you are doing a science activity involving flying objects.

3. You've just found an unlabeled container of white powder that looks like salt in the science lab. Write a short paragraph explaining what you should and should not do with it.

4. Every laboratory should have safety equipment. What kind of safety equipment can be found in your school's classroom laboratory? Create a checklist of safety equipment for a lab experiment involving a beaker of water and a hot plate.

TAKE A QUIZ! ⭐

GLOSSARY

allergic reaction (uh-LUR-jik ree-AK-shuhn)—sneezing, watery eyes, swelling, or rashes caused by contact with plants, animals, or substances

biohazard (BYE-oh-haz-urd)—a biological agent, such as blood or body fluids, that may carry infectious diseases

biologist (bye-OL-uh-jist)—a scientist who studies living things

chemist (KEM-ist)—a scientist who studies or works with chemicals

contaminated (kuhn-TAM-uh-nay-tid)—dirty or unfit for use

corrosive (kuh-ROW-siv)—able to destroy or eat away at something little by little

flammable (FLAM-uh-buhl)—able to burn

germs (JURMS)—small living things that cause disease; bacteria and viruses are two common types of germs.

habitat (HAB-uh-tat)—the place and natural conditions where an animal lives

latex (LAY-teks)—a milky liquid that comes from certain plants; latex is used to make rubber.

poisonous (POI-zuhn-uhss)—able to kill or harm if swallowed, inhaled, or touched

porcelain (POR-suh-lin)—a hard ceramic made by firing and glazing clay

sharps (SHARPS)—knives, needles, and broken glass

specimen (SPESS-uh-muhn)—a sample that a scientist studies closely

READ MORE

Canavan, Thomas. *Extreme Science Experiments*. London, England: Arcturus Publishing Limited, 2018.

Martineau, Barker. *Science Experiments at Home: Discover the Science in Everyday Life.* STEM Starters for Kids. New York: Skyhorse Publishing, 2018.

Snoke Harris, Elizabeth. *Weird and Wonderful Science Experiments Volume 2: Cool Creations: Make Slime, Crystals, Invisible Ink, and More!* Weird and Wonderful Science Series. Minneapolis, Minn.: Quarto Publishing Group USA, 2018.

INTERNET SITES

Use Facthound to find Internet sites related to this book.

Visit *www.facthound.com*

Just type in 9781543529487 and go!

Super-cool stuff! Check out projects, games and lots more at **www.capstonekids.com**

INDEX